W9-BXY-017

I was no more than eight or nine when it had come home to me that the fate of the breathing person was to be hurt and then annihilated.

Robert Fitzgerald,
Notes on a Distant Prospect

For me it is the virgin birth, the Incarnation, the resurrection which are the true laws of the flesh and the physical. Death, decay, destruction are the suspension of these laws. I am always astonished at the emphasis the Church puts on the body. It is not the soul she says that will rise but the body, glorified. I have always thought that purity was the most mysterious of the virtues, but it occurs to me that it would never have entered the human consciousness to conceive of purity if we were not to look forward to a resurrection of the body, which will be flesh and spirit united in peace, in the way they were in Christ. The resurrection of Christ seems the high point in the law of nature.

Flannery O'Connor,
The Habit of Being

Death and the Rest of Our Life

John Garvey

WILLIAM B. EERDMANS PUBLISHING COMPANY
GRAND RAPIDS, MICHIGAN / CAMBRIDGE, U.K.

© 2005 Wm. B. Eerdmans Publishing Co.
All rights reserved

Wm. B. Eerdmans Publishing Co.
255 Jefferson Ave. S.E., Grand Rapids, Michigan 49503 /
P.O. Box 163, Cambridge CB3 9PU U.K.
www.eerdmans.com

Printed in the United States of America

10 09 08 07 06 05   7 6 5 4 3 2 1

Library of Congress Cataloging-in-Publication Data

Garvey, John, 1944-
Death and the rest of our life / John Garvey.
p.   cm.
ISBN 0-8028-2918-X (pbk.)
1. Death — Religious aspects — Christianity.   I. Title.
BT825.G34   2005
236′.1 — dc22

2005047755

Scripture quotations in this publication are from the Revised Standard
Version of the Bible, Old Testament, copyright 1952; New Testament, 2nd
edition, 1971; Apocrypha, copyright 1957; The Third and Fourth Books of
the Maccabees and Psalm 151, copyright 1977 by the Division of Christian
Education of the National Council of the Churches of Christ in the
United States of America. Used by permission. All rights reserved.

In memory of my parents,

Hugh Garvey and Jane Driscoll Garvey

and

for Regina, the greatest gift and blessing

Contents

Acknowledgments

The editors of *Commonweal* asked me for an article on death, and that request happened to coincide with a book I had started to write, but without their request the book would not have become what it is. I am grateful for that invitation, as well as for the many years *Commonweal* has been a place to write from. Thanks also to my brothers and sisters, Joan, Hugh, Ann, Michael, Thomas, Peter, and Patience. Their love and generosity following the death of our parents are a continuing source of joy. Thanks are also due to Fr. Alexander Garklavs and the parishioners at Holy Trinity Orthodox Church, who have given me a kind of harbor from which I can write and occasionally be of service.

Introduction

What does it mean to try to write about death — an experience none of us can know? We watch people dying, but those who watch cannot possibly know what this final thing means — they either have never known anything like it or have always recovered from whatever it was that might have killed them.

Yet death defines our life in profound ways, and not only as a final limit, a boundary. Our fears, our strategies to avoid thinking about death, our desire to control the uncontrollable, or our willingness to look at death honestly will finally make us who we are. It makes sense that great philosophers and religious thinkers have counseled their listeners to contemplate their own deaths on a daily basis. It is also understandable, if not a sign of our wisdom, that most human beings have studiously ignored them.

If we do not ignore them, then we console ourselves with images of an afterlife, considered often as if death meant only a change of scenery or condition. Or we take a philosophical approach: I did not experience anything before my birth; why should I worry about the lack of any life after death?

I want to approach death and dying from a number of angles, trying to show what personal, philosophical, and religious points of view can and cannot do to help us towards an understanding and acceptance of death. Avoiding these questions not only keeps us from leading fuller, more profound and even joyful lives, but neglecting them can poison our days and our relationships with other people.

What I have written comes from several sources: reading, of course; my own experience as someone who has been around a number of deaths as a pastor in an Orthodox church; most of all as someone who has seen the deaths of people I love. I hope that what I offer will be helpful and will lead readers to some clarity and an honest attempt to understand their relationship to a mystery that forms us all.

*　　*　　*

Not very long ago I encountered death in ways that changed me. I had always been the sort of person for whom death formed the backdrop when you took all the distractions away. I nearly died of illness as a child; a grandfather who was a big part of my childhood died when I was twelve; and my sister Grace died at the age of eighteen months when I was fifteen.

All of this, combined with something melancholy in my nature, something probably genetic, made me angry, fearful, anxious, and depressed. This sad, linked combination of weights on the soul was something I wore until my early forties, when much of it lifted. This may be because some important personal decisions (among them the decision to become a member of the Orthodox Church, something I had been circling for years) helped heal the internal divisions; it may also have been the mercy of getting older. Death was still there, a daily companion, but it wasn't accompanied by the same Gnostic sense that the whole universe was wrong, a malign engine for killing the people you love. I could be calm about it.

As an Orthodox parish priest I saw many fami-

3

lies go through the deaths of people they loved. The hardest was the death of a two-year-old, a lively little girl whose parents' marriage was already strained and finally, after her death, came apart in a bitter, ugly way.

Then our twelve-year-old goddaughter suffered a terrible head injury in an automobile accident. Eight days later she died. My wife and I were with her parents when the doctors told them that she would probably not survive, and if she did the damage would be severe. I was in the intensive care unit with her family when the monitors went wild, then flat-lined.

Not long after this my mother died. She had been ill for a while, but she had the kind of illness — congestive heart failure — that made us think she might be with us for a few more years. When we got the news of her death, my wife and I were on the way to be with her. She had already fallen into a coma, and she died while we were on the road. A little more than two years later, my father died. His death was very different: He was diagnosed with a cancer that had metastasized to his liver and bones, and he died at home, with family present, and — thanks to hospice care — relatively free of pain. After a couple of days spent in morphine-induced sleep, he opened his eyes, smiled at my sister, and died.

So I have been aware of death on a daily basis for some time now. It's really more than daily; it is a constant backlighting. This has made me examine the ways in which I have ordinarily responded to death, and to examine the ways many others — religious and nonreligious people alike — have tried to make sense of mortality.

What does it mean to keep death before you? Can't this poison life with a kind of bleakness, draining the moment of any joy? And what good does it do to think about death, since it is in any case inevitable? It will happen whether I am aware of it always or never. Is it even possible to think about death, since — although we can see, and feebly imagine, what it might be like to be dying — death itself is literally beyond us or our imagining?

We often say that religion can console people in the face of death, and to some extent this is true. But some of this consolation is false, and at times religion, or at least certain sorts of religion, can make it less likely that people will encounter death realistically. Superstitious, false uses of religion abound, and as difficult as it may be, since people need consolation, we have good pastoral and personal reasons for trying to keep people from embracing them.

I want to explore some of the ways in which we should allow what death means to illuminate all of our life. My perspective is that of a member and priest of the Orthodox Church, but I do not claim to speak for the church. Some of what I have to say is at odds with the somewhat sentimental and quite non-biblical ways that Christians have typically been taught (more by their cultures than by the church, though the church has often acquiesced) to think about death.

Trying to deal honestly with death seems necessarily uncomfortable, and trying to avoid the discomfort or talk it away seems dishonest. But a serious consideration of death can, strange as it may seem, be a source of joy and hope, if not exactly of comfort. I have opened this book with two quotations, one from the poet and translator Robert Fitzgerald, the other from his good friend Flannery O'Connor. Both were Christians. Fitzgerald's words emphasize the fact that suffering and death are our fate, and someone who does not come to terms with this is in fact living in illusion. O'Connor speaks of resurrection and says that — beyond everything that happens to us this side of death —

we have faith that resurrection is our even truer fate. Both truths — one demonstrable, the other hoped for — need to be held at the same time. The necessary tension between them may produce a human life, as human life is meant to be lived.

Death and the Rest of Our Life

Chapter One

My wife and I visited my father the summer before his death. We live in New York; he lived in Illinois. So we visited, usually once a year, for a week or so. And because we saw him that rarely, we noticed every time we visited how age had changed him. That last summer we saw that his height had diminished; he stooped more; he had a tremor I hadn't noticed before. But at eighty-four he was remarkably lively. His conversation was as funny and passionate as ever. His eyesight had diminished because of macular degeneration, and although he still read, it was a labor. Not being able to read easily was a terrible deprivation: He had been an editor and publisher for almost all of his professional life though he had started out as a reporter for the Cleveland Press (and had a press card signed by Eliott Ness to prove it — Ness had become public safety director in Cleveland after his more colorful Chicago career). When he had to give up driving at last, he hated the loss of independence.

He was in good spirits, but since the death of my mother about two years before our visit, we had felt that he was biding his time, waiting to die. He was not depressed or despairing. He simply felt that his life's work was over; he had seen his children grow up and start their own families; he had grandchildren and great-grandchildren. He loved recalling the parts of his life that involved the friendships formed in and after college, as well as the friends made during his years in publishing, when he worked in New York for Henry Holt and commuted first from Flushing, then from Pelham. During that period he edited Bill Maulden's *Up Front,* made the great mistake of turning down Malcolm Lowry's *Under the Volcano,* and met and corresponded with a number of writers and poets, including Alan Tate, with whom he worked, and Peter Taylor. At Notre Dame he met Henry Rago, a poet and later editor of *Poetry,* who remained a lifelong friend, as was the poet and translator Robert Fitzgerald, whose hometown was Springfield, Illinois, the town our family lived in. After my father moved there and started his own publishing firm, Templegate, he traveled to England to form a kind of alliance with an English firm, Burns Oates, and he met Evelyn Waugh, who visited our home on a U.S. tour. My father loved talking about all of this.

During what we did not know would be our second-to-last visit, he enjoyed cooking with my wife, Regina, and in the evenings he consumed more martinis than I could or wanted to. We noticed him wince with pain on occasion, something he put down to age and arthritis. So did we, at the time. We've since wondered whether this might not have been the first sign of the cancer, which had already metastasized to his bones but was not diagnosed for another six months.

After we returned to New York, we talked about moving back to Springfield to help out. My brothers lived in or near Springfield, but they had work and families of their own. They were very attentive and saw my father often. But as a writer and priest without a parish, I was portable. Regina was less so, but she could find something to do to make a living in Springfield, and we thought it might be helpful to be there. At the same time, we knew that Dad would not want to think that we had rearranged our lives on his account. We put off anything as firm as a decision and waited to see how well he fared.

Since Mom's death I had phoned him every two or three days, and his spirits were usually good, though I noticed in the autumn that he seemed a little more subdued. My brothers and sisters who lived closer to home noticed a physical decline. He was losing weight and seemed less energetic. Medical tests showed a heart arrhythmia, which was corrected with medication, but the weakness and weariness continued. "I don't know what worries me more," my brother Peter, a nurse, told Dad's doctor, "the fact that he's stopped going to Mass every morning or the fact that he's not drinking."

Dad had some more tests at the urging of my brother-in-law Steve, a physician who living in another town who was concerned about a lack of progress towards a diagnosis. A few days before Christmas, Dad was diagnosed as having cancer, which had spread from the pylorus to his bones and liver. When he asked his physician how much time he had left he was told, "A few months. . . ."

"Oh, God, no!"

"Or a few weeks."

"That's better," Dad said.

Regina and I began driving west when we heard. On Christmas Day we arrived in Springfield, which had been hit with a snowstorm. When we got to Dad's hospital room, the first thing he said after we kissed him was, "Well, so far dying's not so bad."

His spirits were good. He knew he could go home soon, that he would die there and not in the hospital. Since my mother's death he had, in a way, been waiting for this. He said that he was not afraid of dying but was concerned about the pain. According to Dad, when he mentioned this to his doctor, the doctor reassured him: "We can deal with that. We'll do what we've done since ancient times . . . we'll put you in the arms of Morpheus." Dad liked that.

We set up a hospital bed in Dad's bedroom and dismantled and stored the bed he and Mom had shared. We bought a comfortable recliner for the living room so Dad could be with us for as long as it was comfortable for him. He seemed resigned and passive, yet at the same time his spirits were good . . . he didn't seem at all depressed. He had no hesitation about asking for help, and he didn't need to be in control. He was still talking with us, even joking, but in some way he was already faced in another direction, and it was not towards us, though he was still with us and happy to be there.

He had been eating little. Now he ate almost nothing, just small bites, bits of candy, sips of water. The hospice nurse had told us, "Keep in mind that he's not dying because he's not eating. He's not eating because he's dying."

We had no way of knowing how long it would be before he died. Regina and I left on a morning when Dad slept later than he usually did since his return from the hospital. It was the beginning of a period in which he slept most of the time. We may have shared one of his last waking days. The night before we left, I read to him from letters my sisters had found, which they had placed in chronological order. They were written by my mother's sister, Mary Driscoll, to her parents. One described a visit my mother made shortly after falling in love with my father. "It was wonderful to have Jane here," she wrote, "and I'll miss her when she leaves, but if she says one more word about Hugh Garvey I'll kill her."

Dad laughed when I read that. During those last days of consciousness, and maybe in ways we can't know even after he was unconscious, he loved having the family around him. One evening after dinner there was a moment of silence. Dad's eyes were closed, as they often were then. We thought he was asleep, but after the silence lasted longer than he liked he said, "Keep talking."

The last two evenings we were with him he received many calls from his sisters (both of his brothers had died), from nieces and nephews and grandchildren, telling him of their love, assuring him of prayers. He managed to handle it all with grace and good humor, but I always had the sense that he had already made his goodbyes. All of us, knowing that there would come a time when we might not know that he could still hear us, spent some time alone with him. On the morning we left, Regina and I waited for him to wake up and then went into his room. It was terrible to know that this would likely be the last time I would see him alive. I told him how grateful I was for the love and great example he and my mother had given to us, and that if I made it through life in a good way and into eternal life, it would be because of them. He smiled and said, "You're a great son. God bless you."

Leaving that room was the hardest thing I've ever done. We left in tears, and the tears continued as we drove away, and they were there off and on all the way back to New York.

I phoned home every day. My sisters Joan and Ann stayed with him, often sleeping in the same room. My father slept most of the time now. One morning a nurse told my sister Ann that she might want to leave the room as she cleaned my father to get him started for the day, but Ann instinctively told her to wait for a while and said she would stay with him. A few minutes later he opened his eyes, looked at her, smiled, and died.

We returned for the funeral, and I returned once again after that to go through the house with my brothers and sisters to divide the property among us. I have seen other families divided by death — years of banked-up bitterness can surface at last and old resentments come out of hiding, but we were blessed with an outpouring of charity and generosity. Following the funeral, on our way back into whatever ordinary living can mean in the face of mortality, grief, and gratitude, we were relieved, even blessed, knowing some joy in the fact that our gratitude was at least as deep as our grief, if not deeper.

I realize now that in his final years my father had to learn to surrender everything, and he did it gracefully, if not easily. The woman he loved and had been married to for fifty-seven years died before he did, and he had more than two years of acute loneliness. He lost his eyesight gradually and with it one of his greatest joys — reading. He also lost an autonomy he had been used to . . . now he had to ask his sons to drive him to the grocery store, to church, to doctors' appointments. They were willing, but he told me this was almost harder than not being able to read. It was difficult to be so dependent. Finally, he lost what he would once have thought of as his dignity, but he moved beyond that notion. The night before I left, he asked me to help him to the bathroom and wait while he settled himself onto the toilet, asking me to make sure that a rug was under his feet to protect him from the floor's cold. He could never have done this before, this nakedness before a child of his, asking for that kind of help; but he had never died before, and he was increasingly turned in the direction of dying, knowing he was leaving everything he had known, and he seemed at peace with it. Part of it, I am sure, was his faith that he would be with my mother, with other people he loved. An even greater part was a firm acceptance of death's inevitability, as well as a belief that whatever lay at the base of his faith was not false. My sister Joan said later, "He taught us how to die."

I am the oldest of eight siblings and, since my parents' death, the oldest member of my immediate family. This gives me the constant sense that I am probably next . . . that is, the next in line to die. This is, of course, not necessarily so. My father's youngest brother was the first of his siblings to die, and my mother outlived her three older siblings. But it seems natural to think this way, and in ways I find surprising, given my lifelong melancholia, it isn't a terrible thought. One of the things that has helped me is seeing the way in which my father was able to accept his own dying. Another is the realization that I have lived to see my two children grow up, marry good people, and have children of their own. The marriage Regina and I have shared is a joy, and I am grateful for many things. But even if this were not the case, my being around death has made it clear to me that the absolute inevitability of death is the most essential fact of our life, the one thing we must be clear about at every stage of life . . . not only our own death, but the fact that everyone we know and love will die. This means that the words we say to others must be said with our mutual mortality in mind. They could be our last. I know one family who fought bitterly before one of them stormed away from the house and died, minutes later, in an auto accident. I share this example, not to make us feel guilty about the words we can't take back, but to develop a realism about our shared lives. One Buddhist manual for monks says that a monk, seeing that all of us are mortal and will suffer before we die, forms "a tender estimate" of the true condition of human beings. It is that tender estimate that should inform all of our behavior. If clarity about this becomes a part of our daily prayer and practice, it will not need to be a constant remembering, any more than we have to remember to breathe.

Chapter Two

Many books have been written about near-death experiences and what they show about life after death, and they have always left me skeptical, perhaps because of my own experience. When I was a child I was seriously ill and was at one point quite close to death. I remember a vivid dream from that time, so vivid it did not seem like a dream, in which I found myself swimming above my body with another ill child, who urged me to swim on. I saw my own body from above, lying still in the hospital bed, and instead of swimming on with my friend, I dived into the bed and woke up. Whether this was a powerful dream, or the effect of oxygen deprivation, or a near-death experience, I can't say. It doesn't prove anything to me, nor do stories about a tunnel of light and other types of near-death experiences.

But there are many stories about what people say as they approach death — stories that come from relatives, from nurses, from chaplains, priests, ministers, rabbis, and others who are near dying people and their families — that show a common set of themes. These stories can be reassuring because they show that dying people often approach the end of life in a way that does not involve fear but acceptance, and in some cases even longing. But we need to view their reassurance with some caution.

One woman, gasping for breath, told me that if the doctors could not make her feel better she was more than ready for death. She was tired of the physical exhaustion she had been experiencing in the effort to live, and she believed her life had been a good one: She had been a widow for years, but she was grateful for a good marriage and for her children, she felt that she had been blessed in friendships, and she thought that it was time to go.

This readiness to die is sometimes expressed, however, in stranger ways — in dreams and in images that suggest that the dying expect to be with those they love, that they expect to be with God, and that they often see this in terms of a passage or journey.

My grandfather died in his mid-nineties and had outlived all but one of his siblings. He told one of his nurses that he missed his family. She was puzzled, because his sons and daughters were in touch with him often and visited frequently. When she mentioned this, he said, "No — I mean I miss my brothers and sisters."

When a nurse friend and I visited an old man who was dying in a nursing home, he spoke frequently of his parents and a younger sister who had died. He had spoken to us often of his family, of their emigration from Istanbul to America. As he approached death his speech was often drifting and confused, but at one point he said, "I'm going to ride a train soon." When we asked him what train he was going to ride, he said, "The one my father rode."

A woman who had wanted to go on a cruise with her husband but had never been able to realize that dream asked her family, who were with her because they knew her death was very close, "What time is it?" "Seven," they answered. "It's too early," she said. "The boat leaves at ten." Her family told me that she died at ten.

A sense of being about to join the beloved dead is common. Shortly before her death, an old woman in my parish told her granddaughter about a dream in which she saw her family gathered in a beautiful field, waiting for her, and she longed to be with them. At one point she tried to get out of the bed — she had been restrained because she frequently tore at the IVs and the lines connecting her to the monitors — and her granddaughter told her she couldn't get up. "But I have to," she said. "You don't understand. I'm getting married today. . . . I'm getting married to God."

It is interesting how often these images take the form of travel, passing from where we are to a beautiful place, sometimes by boat or train, or on foot . . . as if we were hard-wired to think of death as going from one place to another place. A built-in illusion, a comforting lie? Some might say so. Others would argue that we have no reason to think that such images do not point in a real direction. In any case, while these stories taken by themselves prove nothing, they show that dying people often approach death peacefully, and they reassure the families left behind.

Another form of reassurance can be found in the dreams that people often have following the death of a loved one. Occasionally the person who has died will appear in a dream unusual for its clarity and power, and people who have experienced this have told me they are convinced it was the dead person's way of trying to reassure them that he or she is all right, even happy.

I mention all of these stories because they are an important part of the way many people experience the death of people they love. And they are reassuring, in a way; but I think it is important not to depend on them or believe that they are proof of anything other than that life can sometimes be more merciful than we expect it to be. We cannot prove that these are anything more than reassuring illusions nature builds into our dying to make our extinction less terrifying. (Though why would a nature so impersonal as not to give a damn about Alzheimer's disease, birth defects, bipolar disorder, and osteoporosis care to see us comforted at the end?) Nor can we prove that they are anything other than stories we tell ourselves to keep the dark at bay.

In fact, many deaths are not experienced in these reassuring ways; some are simply grueling and painful, not redeemed in any apparent way by any consolation. I remember a bitter man who, after a life of suffering and confinement, experienced a few short years of comfort and independence, only to die of cancer. I was a volunteer in a hospice program and had asked what I could do for him — many people wanted letters written or milkshakes fetched — and he began to shout, "You can't do anything for me! Nobody can!" Years later a parishioner who was dying told me that she was going through a hard time, everything in her felt hard and unyielding and painful, but, she said, "It's because I am a hard woman." And she was, in fact. She thought her hard death was connected to that, and it was hard to the end. Other deaths involve families gathered around a bed in which someone unconscious is on a ventilator until the heart monitor shows a flat line. Some good conversation and reminiscence among the family might happen during those long hours; often they face simply an agonizing time, a long waiting.

The comforting stories can be misleading in the way some faith healers are. When a dying child is not healed, some might say it is because the parents lacked faith or were not praying with enough wholeheartedness and trust. Such words make them feel guilt for something truly beyond them. Similarly, these stories of comfort, impressive as they are, and as grateful as we may be if they happen to occur in our lives, can lead people who do not have such experiences to think that they have somehow failed as sons, daughters, husbands, wives, lovers, and friends. Why should this happen to my friend Jim and not to me? For some, the death of someone loved is neither accompanied by reassuring words from the dying person nor followed by a comforting dream. It is simply loss, loss deep down, the knowledge that on this side of death I will not be with this person I loved anymore, nor she with me.

Even if powerful and reassuring experiences are grounded in something real (and whether they are or not cannot be proved), we should view their absence as something other than simple deprivation. This apparent darkness may be a call to a deeper trust, a trust not in one's own lived experiences, as valuable as those may be, but a trust in God's faithful word. Whatever our experience — or lack of any consoling experience at all — we must finally put our trust in the God whose Son's last words include the terrible question, "My God, my God, why have you forsaken me?" (Matt. 27:46).

Jesus' willingness to go even to the place where God cannot go, a place where there is no life, his absolute obedience and submission — this was, and is now, the beginning of resurrection. In the letter to the Philippians, Paul speaks of Christ's self-emptying, first of any "equality with God" (2:6), and then, having taken on our humanity, through an obedience that leads to death on the cross. "Therefore" — as a result of this emptying, not a reward for it, but precisely because of it — "God has highly exalted him" (2:9). Paul tells us to "have this mind among yourselves" (2:5). For us, self-emptying can mean accepting in this moment a sense of complete forsakenness, believing that Christ has gone there before us and that, trusting and hoping in God, we may rise through that absolute darkness into an unimaginable joy.

Chapter Three

When I had been a parish priest for only a couple of years, I was at the bedside of a woman who had returned from the hospital to die in her home. She felt no pain but was weary to the bone, ready to die, tired of the wasting illness she had been going through for a long time, but she was still anxious. Knowing that I had never been where she was, and not wanting to say something banal at this crucial time, I was left in a sort of stammering place. I said the meager things I could, anointed her, and gave her communion. I told her that she was about to encounter what we had talked about, what we had celebrated in the sacraments of the church. I really felt helpless to say anything else; she had suffered in ways I had not. Moments before I left her side she said, softly, "I just hope it's true."

At one level, that's it. It comes down to that: I hope it's true. We have — can have — no proof other than what we are told in the letter to the Hebrews: "Now faith is the assurance of things hoped for, the conviction of things not seen" (11:1). This involves trust, whatever our feelings or the depths of conviction might be. The feeling of the dying person may range from total, deeply held conviction to a kind of hanging on with the fingernails.

Let us be clear about what we can understand — and cannot — understand here. We must not allow a sentimental picture of death to form our understanding, for then a real encounter with death will stagger us; and, because our hope has been so badly grounded, we may then lose all hope. Also, we should not walk away from any consideration of what is finally a mystery on the grounds of its unknowability. Singer Iris Dement has an appealing agnostic hymn (that's all that I can call it) about the different speculations people have about the afterlife; the refrain suggests that she will simply let the mystery be. This expresses an entirely proper unknowing; but the problem is, the mystery won't let *us* be. From prehistoric burial practices through the Gilgamesh epic to the present, we have faced a question — perhaps the most basic human question — which the theologian John Dunne puts this way: "If I must someday die, what can I do to satisfy my desire to live?"[1]

There are many answers, good and bad, profound and glib: transcend it, realize that it isn't the right question, let go of the desire. And modern society offers the almost comical technological solution: freeze your body cryonically until science comes up with a cure for what killed you or with a recipe for bodily immortality.

But however you approach the question, or fail to approach it, your response will form not only your opinion about death but also the ways in which you approach the rest of your life, the ways that you enjoy the moment or make decisions about moral questions or appreciate a work of art, and the ways you live with other people. How we approach death tells us what we think human beings are called to be in this life. This has to do with much more than what has been called "the promise of an afterlife." That's part of the question, but there is much more.

Some questions are finally so mysterious, so un-

1. John Dunne, *City of the Gods* (New York: Macmillan, 1965), pp. v, 217.

knowable, that we cannot approach them systematically. We can know something about dying — we have seen it, and many of us have come uncomfortably close. About death itself we know only that we cannot imagine it, really, except to sense that dying means leaving everything we know and can know. This mystery not only darkens our understanding of life; it also illuminates it.

*   *   *

From the earliest human times, the ways in which people regarded and tended to their dead have marked us uniquely among species. (Evidence shows that some other higher mammals know grief and even respond to places associated with the death of their kind; but it is as if you were comparing a tune of two or three notes with a symphony, where other animals and humans are concerned.) In what is now Iraq, the body of a Neanderthal man was discovered, buried in a fetal position — leaving the world in the way he was born — and covered with yarrow flowers and daffodils. The various elaborate ways people have been buried or ritually exposed; the tribal patterns in which speaking of the dead is taboo; the sharp contrasts between the

34

Egyptian efforts at preserving the bodies of dead royalty and the reverent but swift preparation of the unembalmed body by Jews and Muslims; cremation in Hindu funeral practice — all of these say that death is about something more than the simple ending of life on this Earth. It has to do with the mystery and meaning of that life.

The book of Tobit tells us that Tobit, in defiance of the Assyrian rulers, gave food and clothing to the needy and buried Hebrews murdered by their oppressors. Even after informers turned him in, he continued this practice. When he learned of the murder of one Hebrew, he said, "I returned from burying him, and because I was defiled I slept by the wall of the courtyard . . ." (Tobit 2:9).

His pious act, preparing someone for burial, touching a dead man, defiles him. What makes someone ritually unclean is often misunderstood. The word "unclean" is unfortunate, because it implies something filthy or lowly. But when you look at the things that make one unclean in Jewish practice — corpses, blood in sex or in food, semen — you see that they have to do with the sources and the limits of life or with the fact of death. In other words, they have to do with the boundaries of the sacred, with those things that are in God's hands and not in ours. You do not move from these realms into ordinary life without a need for purification, something that marks a sense of real transition from the sacred to the mundane.

The sacred is not just a sentimental category. It removes us from the ordinary, the secular — that is, the daily, having to do solely with the present age or present time. The shock at the start of Camus's *The Stranger* is that death is dealt with as if it were not sacred but "mere": "Today mother is dead. Or maybe yesterday; it doesn't matter." This attitude is a violation, and Camus knew it.

Much religious and secular thought has been expended in the effort to make death "mere." The words "death is just a part of life" trip too easily off too many tongues. People tell stories of those who die well or peacefully to reassure us, understandably, but these people have nothing at stake here. I have seen what I can only call "good deaths." (It is ironic that the word "euthanasia," translated literally, means "good death." In our time a good death is apparently one we control. But of course, death is not controlled by euthanasia, but only some aspects of dying.) I have also seen deaths that were drawn out and difficult. However, more often I have seen, at funerals and in discussions at coffee hours after church, a rush towards a sentimental view of death. The horrible things people say to grieving people are revealing. For instance, I've heard people say to a woman whose child has just died, "God must have wanted her in heaven," and "I know you'll get over this." Worst of all they say: "At least you have the other two," and "You can always have another one." One grieving woman said to me, "I don't doubt that Anna is with God. I only know that she's not with me." The clichés she had to endure went into her like knives. She knew they were well intended, but knowing that didn't help much.

These shallow responses to death not only mark an inability to consider seriously something inevitable in all of our lives, an honest encounter that is demanded of us, but they also signal our need for illusion, for idols. Simone Weil wrote, "Love is not consolation. It is light."[2] Death must be encountered as it is, not as we want it to be.

Before trying to approach what death is, we must recognize the ways we evade it — because this can give us the beginning of an approach to what it is.

2. Simone Weil, *Gravity and Grace* (London: Routledge, 1997), p. 55.

Here's one way we evade it while trying to understand it: "I've been a good person — why is this happening to me?" The Hindu *Mahabarata* offers this ancient riddle: Why is it that people, who see others dying all around them every day, are astonished when they realize that they themselves have to die? Clearly, we have learned nothing from time or history. Built into this attitude is the idea that a certain sort of living will cushion the blow or avert death altogether: If I am good, God/karma/fate will reward me, and I will not suffer, nor will those I love.

Many people approach religion in a way that can only be called superstitious. Indeed, if it weren't for their superstition they would probably abandon religion as of no value. If I am not rewarded for my good behavior and church attendance, why bother with it at all? What is the point of believing in anything, if this allegiance is of no practical value to me?

I have encountered this superstitious attitude when talking with people who have learned that they have cancer or whose family members are suffering: How could God do this to me? I try to live ethically and I go to church. The "why me?" phenomenon is everywhere. If we point out that Jesus (who certainly lived a good life) also suffered, the superstitious person usually responds, "It was different for him. He was divine." Or, "He had to" — the implication being, "and I don't." Religion at this level is not much different from carrying a rabbit's foot for good luck. This common attitude reveals a naivety about suffering and death, one that distorts the biblical idea that sin and human suffering and death are connected. This idea pervades the Old Testament, and Paul writes in Romans 5:12, "[S]in came into the world through one man, and death through sin, and so death spread to all men because all men sinned."

We need to challenge the "why me?" approach, not by scorning it but by elevating it. We need to make it a communal question rather than a personal one. In what kind of universe do the just suffer and the wicked prosper? And in which both die anyway? The answers can range from Gnosticism to atheism, but they can also lead to the book of Job (which is not an answer but which deepens the question) or to the cross.

Let's pay some attention to this. The connection between the death represented by the cross and sin is not obvious. It isn't at all philosophically satisfying or demonstrable. Sin itself is not. But consider the fact that we might not see our situation for what it is precisely because of the pervasive tragedy of our situation. We grow old enough to reproduce and then move towards death, which usually comes after a period of decline and some pain. The universe we can see and measure is indifferent to our suffering. This implies that our suffering has no meaning for us other than our having washed up here, no meaning other than our abandonment in this sad state; this is the atheist response, and some of the resulting ethic has a noble edge. Since the universe doesn't give a damn about compassion, we must, since we are able to. But this is as unsatisfying as any superstitious religious response. Indeed, it *is* a religious response of sorts.

Atheists often say that the idea of a loving God, a God who loves us like a father or mother, is not compatible with a universe in which suffering is so much a part of every conscious, and even unconscious, life. This apparent gulf is not a stupid concern. People can use it to try to end all thinking about God. Suffering pervades reality. Therefore, we might conclude, there is no loving, benevolent God. But this also deepens the concept of God and our relationship to God, as the book of Job does, as does the cross, where God may be said in some sense to suffer with the creation within which suffering is inevitable.

Neither believers nor nonbelievers take the problem of suffering and God as seriously as it should be taken. For instance, much of the most hideous suffering is certainly inflicted by human beings upon other human beings. This makes a better argument for the religious idea of a fallen humanity than an argument against God. But many hideous forms of suffering are inflicted by creation itself. In Genesis we read, "And God saw everything that he had made, and behold, it was very good" (1:31). Is it? A child is born without a brain, a young woman contracts ALS, a loved father fades away with Alzheimer's, old people are plagued with pain. . . . How can we affirm that such a universe is good when suffering is so pervasive? The universe is beautiful and awe-inspiring in many ways, but *good?* That's not apparent. At least, as we ordinarily define goodness it is not.

Believers from Old Testament times to the present have said that suffering has entered creation because of sin. This is a truly unsatisfying assertion. How could this be so? How could my sin possibly justify or make more understandable the terrible fear experienced by a person with schizophrenia, or

41

the pain of a child dying of leukemia, or the sorrow of her parents? To say that sin causes suffering is plainly not an explanation or a logical argument. It is meant to be taken as a statement of fact, but it can't be argued towards logically any more than a hailstorm can be. We observe that suffering is universal, that evil in this sense is real, that the fear of death drives us to hatred and hoarding, that to exist is to suffer, that we will finally lose everything we love. To assert (another non-argument), in the face of suffering, that God is good and that creation was from the beginning meant to be good is to say that a catastrophe has happened and creation has somehow been twisted away from its true meaning.

The Gnostic explanation for the catastrophe is to deny that the author of the physical world is a good God; the creator is the Demi-urge, something inferior to the good God, something perhaps crazed or evil. A good God exists, but not here, and this catastrophe is not that God's work.

This makes a kind of sense until I look at a child, at all that is wonderful in the world, and then see that creation is both profoundly good and wounded beyond our understanding. The fact that it takes the incarnation, the crucifixion, and the resurrection to cut into the ice around our hearts shows the depths of the catastrophe. And the fact that the catastrophe is often more apparent to us than the goodness of creation is not the way God wanted things to be.

To speak of a connection between sin and death is one thing; to think that we can control the consequences of having been born into a broken world — indeed, that we can avoid the consequences — is the point at which religious thinking becomes superstitious, a form of magic, a way we avoid facing death head on.

Philosophy and religion have given many varied, often contradictory, ways of trying to understand death's significance. From ancient times, people have given the atheistic or agnostic response: It can't be known, and to worry about it is futile. Since you have gone away like the flame of a blown-out candle, there will be no *you* left to experience the loss we imagine we will know at death. You have no more reason to fear death or to contemplate it with anxiety than you have to look with anxiety or apprehension at the period before your birth.

One problem with this response is that, in the meantime, I *was* born and came to know and love people and places, food and drink, lovemaking and jokes. . . . To contemplate leaving all of this with no sense of loss or longing requires a hardening of the heart. Clearly, clinging to life also is futile. One by one those we love die, before or after us. Our love for them may be a real and central part of our lives, but it protects them no more than it protects us. We gain a necessary wisdom in learning not to cling to what we love, in realizing that what we love is not, because we love it, possessed and made permanent; but we also gain in this understanding a built-in grief and sorrow, which seems central to being human.

A committed Christian theologian I know said that if he were not a Christian he would be a Buddhist. He is not at all unorthodox as a Christian; he simply felt that outside of Christianity, Buddhism made more sense than any other accounting for the way the world is and the way we are. Christianity and Buddhism both place the question of suffering at the center of their beliefs. Their responses to the question, though ultimately different, share surprising areas of agreement. Unlike some other religious and philosophical approaches to suffering and death, these two faiths make no attempt to explain the mystery away or make it less pointed.

At least this is true of serious Christianity and

serious Buddhism. Buddhism says that suffering is overcome when desire no longer attaches us to the illusion that the self is a subsistent thing. (It says much more than this, but this is an essential part of the message.) Christianity says that suffering is not so much overcome as lived through, and that the final truth is resurrection — but not before suffering and death have been encountered. Death is not the end; resurrection and life — as God wants it to be, not the life of the world wounded by sin — are the true human destinies.

However, we spend much of our life trying to avoid what death means, to make sure that when others die we will not be too wounded, and that we ourselves will not take our own death seriously.

A woman I know approached death in what she thought of as a religiously pious way. After her son died in an accident, she said she felt no grief at all — she knew he was with God and was therefore happy. Her husband didn't feel that way at all, and I couldn't help wondering how hard he must have found it to live with her. It is impossible not to grieve the loss of the loved one's presence, and a lack of grief can call the genuineness of love into question. This is more than a matter of feelings, which are complicated during the time surrounding the death of someone we love. I know people who have been concerned over how little grief they have felt in the immediate aftermath of a death. When my young goddaughter died after lingering eight days in the intensive care unit, I was emotionally drained, and my own exhaustion was connected with concern for her parents and brother. When my mother died unexpectedly and so close to our goddaughter's death, I felt numb — saddened, of course, because I would never talk with her again. But I did not feel the grief I had expected to feel when a parent died. A little more than two years later, my father died, and I realized that as long as he was alive, in some strange sense my mother lived as well — this may have to do with the mystery of the two being one flesh. With his death they were truly gone, both of them, and my grief was much more powerful.

The depth and intensity of feelings that gather around a death can be unsettling. So can the lack of a feeling you expected to have. You find that during a period of mourning the emotions shift. One moment, you think you have learned to accept the death of someone you loved, and then the next you are blindsided by intense grief and longing for the presence of the one who is gone forever. When you experience the death of someone you loved, you do not find "closure" — an overworked, even unnecessary word if ever there was one. In most circumstances you learn to live with grief, but it never goes away completely.

At the same time, we do learn to live with it. And more: We must learn from it as well. What lessons can we learn from grief, from knowing that the people we love will die and we will mourn them, or that we will die and they will mourn us? All of us rejoice when we see a couple who have been well-married, whose lives have known a deep sharing. But one of the tragedies built into the best marriages is that in most cases one person dies before the other, and the loneliness and sorrow that follow for the other are intense. I have talked with a number of men and women (mostly women, who are more commonly the survivors) who have experienced the death of a spouse after a long and good marriage. All feel the loss keenly and suffer intensely from it; and all agree that the years of loving and being loved were a blessing. If the alternative to their present suffering meant never having known such love, all of them would choose the suffering. The mystery of deep love on this side of death involves suffering, as if suffering were built into the nature of love.

The word "compassion," at its root, means "feeling with" and "suffering with." Love always involves compassion. It is easier to suffer pain yourself than to watch someone you love suffer. You wish, in such a situation, to be able to suffer in the other's place, as if that could somehow relieve the pain of the loved one. In the end, losing the company of the loved one brings intense suffering; but it is not as if avoiding love means avoiding suffering. It means only being deprived, in the course of a life that will inevitably involve suffering, of one of the graces that gives meaning and depth and joy to life. Seeing love in the context of mortality — remembering that love is passing, even as we rejoice in it — can make us more sensitive to the other person, less inclined towards taking the other for granted or towards being less attentive to the other than we should be.

Understanding life as something necessarily limited, necessarily entwined with morality, affects every aspect of life, not only love and the loss of loved ones. How we respond to mortality, or fail to respond to it, will influence everything from friendship and marriage to the ways we approach possessions and ambitions, and ultimately our relationship to God.

Chapter Four

But is there any comfort to be found?
Man is in love and loves what vanishes,
What more is there to say?

W. B. Yeats,
Nineteen Hundred and Nineteen

A pervasive consciousness of death marks us as human. From our earliest literature — the ancient Babylonian Gilgamesh epic, for example, where Gilgamesh is tormented by the death of his wild friend, Enkidu, and pursues the hope of immortal life — we have been haunted by the question of what our mortality means, and how we are to respond to it. Our memory focuses not only on what we have loved, but also on what we fear and have not yet experienced personally — and we know it waits for us. We may not have suffered yet, but we can be fairly sure that we will. We know, certainly, that death awaits us, and with death, the unknown. What we have never known before will finally triumph. We may conceive of it as the end of all knowing and the end of the possibility of knowing, a dark beyond dark; we may hope that it will not be that, that a light we cannot now understand will illuminate all of the mystery of what we are and are meant to be. In any case, it is, right now, not knowable. And with that unknowing comes some understandable fear.

Our anticipated encounter with death may be, at a level that informs the rest of our life, something that prepares us for more than death, prepares us for the stages of life that enrich and deepen us and enable us to see life as a whole, something we inhabit without owning it, something we hold without controlling it, something we finally give up, even offer up.

Fear of the unknown is a buried fear of death itself. After all, what you don't know *can* hurt you. Prejudice — judging before the facts are in — is in one sense a reasonable defense mechanism. The stranger who looks and acts in unfamiliar ways may in fact be out to get you, may be an enemy. More than one tribe has as its name for itself "the humans," meaning, of course, that all the other tribes do not quite make the mark. The familiar and accustomed console us; the unfamiliar can seem threatening precisely because we do not know what to expect of it. Children are often afraid of what they are not familiar with. A sentimental falsehood says that children need to be taught hate and prejudice. In fact, they need to be taught civility and tolerance, which do not come naturally but are the hard-won products of civilization.

At the same time, something in us is thrilled by the idea of moving out, of heading for the unfamiliar. The same child who is cautious and afraid to leave his mother's side at one moment will be tempted to run away from home, to explore an unfamiliar place, to see whether that strange house at the end of the block really is haunted. When, at the end of *Huckleberry Finn,* Huck says, "But I reckon I got to light out for the Territory ahead of the rest," something in every reader's heart thrills. We know what he means. The spirit of exploration and escape is not confined to the early explorers or astronauts; it has to do with more ordinary undertakings, like serious friendship, marriage, parenthood.

And undertaken as they should be, they engender a sense of sacredness along with the risk; or, if they do not evoke this at the start, the sacred is revealed as the journey continues. I once met a Russian cosmonaut who had spent months in space and said he would return to space if he could; he found the experience profound and filled with wonder. He said that although no priests went into space, two of his fellow cosmonauts entered the ministry after their return to Earth.

The quest for the sublime in art, we are told, means coming to the edge of a kind of abyss, to a point at which beauty can be so intense as to approach terror. Rilke saw the connection between beauty, terror, and death. Stephen Mitchell's translation of Rilke's first Duino Elegy reads, "For beauty is nothing/but the beginning of terror, which we still are just able to endure,/and we are so awed because it serenely disdains/to annihilate us."[1]

The unknown both frightens us and draws us, and it is associated with both beauty and destruction. Our ideas of divinity are bound up in this un-

1. Rainer Maria Rilke, *The Duino Elegies,* trans. Stephen Mitchell (Boston: Shambhala Publications, 1992).

derstanding. The Bible tells us that no one can look upon the face of God and live. God's answer to Job, which begins, "Where were you when I laid the foundation of the earth?" (38:4), appalls and thrills us at the same time — it is not only powerful but also beautiful. The sense we have of its truth is the sense we have when we view stunning images of the Horsehead Nebula or of the Earth seen over the horizon of the moon.

The unknown, and the possibility of experiencing the sublime, and the fear of losing everything, all show up again and again in the course of our lives. The risks involved in such common but enormous decisions as marriage, parenthood, and the demands of serious friendship are all in some ways linked to the way we understand and respond to our mortality, and our responses can take healthy and unhealthy forms.

From ancient times, the two most common responses to mortality have been sharply at odds. The first is familiar (and it seems to be the one our culture still endorses): "Eat, drink, and be merry, for tomorrow we die." Experience what pleasure you can, because time is fleeting. The important thing, from this point of view, is gratification, satisfaction of every desire. The second response is found in

Stoic and Platonic philosophy: Die before you die. Live ascetically and learn to be detached, knowing that what matters is not what passes and dissolves even as we watch, but eternity.

We may find a third response in what the Orthodox tradition calls "guarding the heart." Pay attention to what happens in the moment, knowing that it is passing, and to the moment's pleasure or pain; see how it affects you. Instead of being moved in one direction or another by passion, by fear or pleasure or pain, observe the feeling and do not let it be the source of your action. But it is supremely important, from the Christian point of view, not to discount the created world or to see it as inferior to some imagined eternity. Our concrete love for particular people matters deeply, and the more deeply we understand what our love means — our love for parents, brothers and sisters, husbands and wives, children and friends — the more we will understand how mortality can either instruct us in love, or lead us to a kind of grasping that ultimately is not compassionate, not at all loving.

I realized something about both trust and the ferocity of love when our first child was born two months prematurely, and for several weeks it was not clear whether she would live. When I first looked at Maria, I realized with an intensity I had never known before that I would die to keep her alive, and I also knew that, except for the constant prayers we were saying, her survival was out of our hands. It was out of our hands even with the prayers, but the prayers were as necessary and natural as breathing. We had to trust, and since I had already experienced the death of a baby sister, I knew as my parents had, offering prayers themselves years before, that trust might not lead us to a place we wanted to be. It was important in that moment to know both fierce love and the need to trust, as well as that neither was something my will could control. I could only pay close attention.

Fear leads us to need to control our lives — fear for ourselves and for those we love. We want to live with the assurance that we will encounter only the expected and the safe, that we will not know any pain. And of course, this desire is both understandable and utterly unrealistic. We will know both unexpected pain and unexpected pleasure. Fear leads us to hoard, to be ungenerous to those in need (What if I give something away and then need help myself? Better to hold on to my money . . .), to be suspicious of the motives of others. Fear keeps us from loving another person without holding something in reserve — what if this person betrays us? What if my child makes choices I do not approve of, or my wife or husband changes after marriage in ways I hadn't expected? What we often think of as love is a grasping at unrealistic security, expecting the one we say we love to make us feel wanted or needed, to remove our loneliness and isolation. And when the other does not provide these things, we are disappointed, even angry: If you loved me you would make me well, heal my loneliness, make me feel important and needed.

Fear is understandable, because given what we have seen of life, our own life and the lives of others, we know that we can be hurt and can lose everything. But it is less apparent that continuing attempts to shore up our security, our egos, our safety, are finally doomed to fail. We will, in fact, ultimately lose it all. A serious spirituality has to take this into account, with the faith that what we receive will be much greater than what we are tempted to retain — but we must also understand that we cannot and should not try to imagine what we will receive (this is a way of trying to have something we can't have). We can only live in the hope and expectation that the promises we have been given are true.

Our faith in those promises can be a means of transformation. To enter marriage, for example, too cautiously, having to negotiate everything, can poison the union from the start. I must be willing to meet the other *as other,* that is, not someone who exists to make me happy or to heal me. The same can be said of serious friendship and of parenthood. All deep relationships require trust and forgiveness. And trust, finally, is learned best when we are serious about our mortality. Trust also means that we will not always know what to expect from the relationship. We may be pleasantly or unpleasantly surprised. But the willingness not to be in control, not to know everything, to learn from the experience as it changes before us, is the beginning of wisdom for living in a world that changes and dies even as it springs to life and grows in front of us.

Dealing with our own death or the death of loved ones becomes particularly difficult when we consider suicide and euthanasia. The two must be considered together because they are, in a sense, two sides of the same coin: the control of the time of death. I suggest that the way we deal with controlled death says everything about the way we see the rest of our lives.

First, consider Dostoyevski's famous statement:

"If God is not real, then all is permitted."[2] This is often taken to mean, "If there is not a God who punishes bad behavior, then people will do anything they like and anarchy will result." This shallow, secular understanding sees religion as a means of social control, with little utility other than that. It assumes that religion is primarily a means of enforcing a point of view. This idea does not take religion seriously as an understanding of the way things are; it dismisses religion in advance.

But Dostoyevski, who said of his faith that his hosannah of belief was forged in the crucible of great doubt, meant something much more profound. (Dostoyevski, after all, argued through Father Zosima in *The Brothers Karamazov* that even the damned are in God's presence; their damnation is their inability to love in return, even in God's presence, a fate they brought on themselves.) He meant that if there is no final meaning to life, then any behavior is equal to any other. This has less to do with punishment than with the leveling of everything, the abolition of any value. A good atheistic

2. This is actually a summary of an argument made by Ivan Karamazov. See Fyodor Dostoevski, *The Brothers Karamazov*, trans. Richard Pevear and Larissa Volkhonsky (San Francisco: North Point Press, 1990), pp. 69-70.

argument can be made that since compassion is absent from the physical universe, we are its only conceivable agents, and therefore we must be merciful to one another. But a good argument against what might be called this Boy Scout atheism — one made by some followers of Nietzsche and all serious followers of the Marquis de Sade — is "Why bother to be merciful?" Why not do what you will, whatever gives you pleasure, since it will all vanish in any event, and the greatest act of mercy will be no more interesting or important or remembered than a sneeze, when the universe has collapsed or imploded or become whatever it will become, in the billions of years after the last human memory has been annihilated by death? And since it is all ultimately without inherent meaning, why not do whatever consoles or pleases you now, whatever makes you comfortable in the moment?

If the only deep value to be found in the universe is the one I place there by my own valuing, if moral value and meaning are not really found in the universe but are placed there unilaterally by human beings, without whom morality and meaning signify nothing, who alone define morality — if there is no moral value intrinsic in the universe, then there is no reason at all that I should not call

all the shots. Why shouldn't I decide how or whether to deal with it? Why shouldn't I decide that the suffering I feel, or that my comatose father or mother feels, should be ended with an injection right now? Or why not abort a child I have not chosen for life? Both the Boy Scout and Marquis de Sade atheists share this understanding.

Religious beliefs (including agnosticism and atheism) have consequences in the larger world. They are not merely matters of private taste, harmless matters of subjective opinion, although this is what secularists would like them to be. Just as atheism or agnosticism can lead to profound ethical conviction — as it did in the case of Albert Camus, for example — it can also lead to great evil, as in the cases of Pol Pot and Stalin. Christianity can lead to heroism, as it did among some French Protestants and Polish Catholics and Bulgarian Orthodox who protected Jews during the Nazi terror, but it can also be lethal, as in the case of the Inquisition and pogroms. Religion can be used to allow us to do whatever we wish to do; politics can be used in the same way. But unlike most other forms of association and belief, religion can also inspire great heroism and self-sacrifice.

This may be because religion, defined as our

deepest understanding of our place in the universe and the reasons (or lack thereof) for our being here, finally has to do with mortality. "Nothing so wonderfully concentrates the mind as the threat of hanging," as Dr. Johnson said. Humans are the only creatures who know their mortality as a defining reality. We are formed, deeply, by how we relate to our . . . what? Extinction? Rebirth? Eternal glory or damnation? To what we believe we will become on the other side of something we fear, to this experience which is in a profound way unknowable to us, and yet is as real as the horizon (and as relative, changing as we approach it), to what will determine how we see the time left to us between now and that unimaginable then.

People commonly believe that a religious belief system, especially a dominant religion, powerfully forms the whole of the culture it inhabits. Some have suggested that much of India's poverty has been influenced by the idea of karma: A person living in misery is reaping the fruits of the evils committed in a previous life; coming to that person's aid is, in a way, beside the point. The idea of fate — everything happens because God has willed it to be that way — has drawn many Islamic societies towards a similar stasis. Christians have boasted that hospitals are the result of a Christian understanding of compassion. Enemies of Christianity have also charged that the misery of the poor in some Christian societies has been tolerated because Christianity teaches that peoples' rewards would come in heaven, so why worry about what happens in this vale of tears? All of these arguments have a certain force, but it is weak, because we can find counterexamples. For instance, while it is true that the charities undertaken by some Hindu groups (especially those inspired by Ramakrishna) were instructed by the example of western Christian charities, the point is that from within their own tradition Hindus saw that charity was a good, even necessary thing. Charity has long been one of the pillars of Islam, as well. And Christians in the west learned mutual tolerance from people who were originally inspired by the secular thinkers of the Enlightenment.

So the influence of religion, even in cultures where one religion is dominant, can be permeated by other influences, often benign, sometimes not. Our own varied and secular society is perhaps the first in history in which the only things that unite us are the things that are there to distract us: politics of the shallowest sort, entertainment, and advertising. This secularization makes it easy for people to argue that the values of all great religious traditions are equally irrelevant, which is the upshot of making religion an entirely private, individual matter. In arguments involving both the origins and end of life, any assertion that life is sacred is met with the counterclaim that to try to follow through on what this might mean is to impose your religious views on others. But this really means that the secular, desacralized universe, the universe in which society alone assigns value, is assumed to be the real one. This is why in the battle over abortion, euthanasia, and capital punishment there can be no shared understanding between the secular and religious. These viewpoints share so little regarding why we are here and what our lives are about that there can be no agreement, only a continual talking past each other. People who are pro-choice in matters of euthanasia and abortion regard those who oppose them as people who might be nice in many ways, but who have an essentially benighted, medieval view of the world; and pro-life people often regard their opponents as very civil, pleasant cannibals.

It is easy to see why people who believe that there is no meaning inherent in the universe would seek to control the circumstances of their lives as fully as possible. Why allow the cold processes of a meaningless, if awesome, universe to determine the course of our lives, when we might be able to enforce an alternative, one that seems more humane, less terrible? So an issue like stem cell research becomes part of the debate. If by manipulating a tiny bit of matter — human matter, yes, but it has not yet become sentient — we may find something that will let us live longer, why not do so? To refuse is to surrender lives to early extinction. To argue against using stem cells to prolong life — to argue that human life in its beginning is sacred, worthy of respect and not to be regarded in such a coldly utilitarian manner — is considered obscurantist and anti-scientific. But such a scientistic approach to life (that is, the view that reduces everything to what can be weighed, measured, and predicted) lacks any serious sense of the tragic. No matter how much we can fix, something will, eventually, kill us. If our life means nothing other than its continuing — and that is something of value only to the one who wishes to go on living — this is indeed a tragedy, and worse than tragedy, because tragedy can teach a lesson. There is no lesson in meaninglessly prolonging life. There really cannot be any final tragedy or joy in a universe in which meaning is assigned by creatures who are themselves aimed towards extinction.

Coming to terms with the limits of life, and the proper limits of what we should feel entitled to do in order to save our lives, is every bit as important as — indeed, more important than — a merely scientific understanding of what we can do.

But if there is a meaning, however mysterious and unnameable, to the fact of our being — a meaning that has to do with the love we have for one another, the desire to live in the face of the inevitability of death, the hope that we are not mistaken to think that the love we have for one another and for the joy we have encountered in one another, and in beauty, is grounded in what the universe is about — this meaning will show itself in the way we cherish what is passing without trying to grasp it.

Our great problem here is forgetfulness. I live in New York City. During the days after September 11, 2001, it was a different, gentler place. There was a quietness I had never experienced here, a kind of tenderness between strangers. Everyone noticed it. The reminders of the event were there every day, not only on the radio and the television stations we could get (several were off the air because their transmitters had been on the World Trade Center towers), but on subways, on the streets, in shops and stores, in offices. Two days after the collapse of the towers, the stench blew into my part of Queens, and I wondered not only what I was inhaling, but who. When I mentioned this, my sister Joan said there was something almost sacramental about that, and I believe there was, in a dark way. I have never felt such solidarity in a common mourning.

Then, a couple of weeks after the horror of that day, I heard a driver shout an obscenity at another, and I thought, "We're back to normal." In a way, it was a relief, but it was also profoundly sad, because we were already starting to forget.

The word for the canon of the Orthodox liturgy, the point at which Jesus' institution of the Eucharist is remembered, is "anamnesis," which is often translated "remembering." But the Greek literally means "against forgetting." This is the task: not to forget, to remember. The advice of so many ancient philosophers and religious thinkers — to keep your own death before you daily — is not only reasonable but also essential. And this should be part of our daily prayer and meditation, not to make us morbid or gloomy, but to lead us to appreciate how fleeting our time is. Many who know that they are terminally ill have said that this knowledge makes them vividly aware of the preciousness of the time they have left; they savor every moment, and waste none of them. The practice of constantly remembering our death should make us more compassionate: If we remember that all of us share this condition, a mixed one in Christian understanding — the terrible fruit of sin and the fall, but also the way into a resurrected life — we will be more careful to refrain from making harsh judgments and saying things that we may never be able to apologize for.

Theologian John Dunne entitled one of his books *The Way of All the Earth*. Mortality and its many ways of affecting us have figured strongly in his approach to theology, and this title was particularly well-chosen: It refers to the passages in Joshua and 1 Kings in which Joshua and David say of their own deaths, "I am about to go the way of all the earth" (Josh. 23:14; 1 Kings 2:2). To go through a day without understanding that what we see and experience is passing, that its nature is to be passing, is to fail to appreciate it, even in a way a failure to love it. And it is by loving what we see and experience, by appreciating it, that we join with God, who saw that what he had made was very good. The greatest art has celebrated this, even if the artist may not have been aware that this is what he was about; but even simple consciousness, when it is awake, is part of this celebration, this love of the world we have been chosen for.

Chapter Five

The first time I seriously questioned what we usually think of as the self, or the soul, was after I had an operation that required an anesthetic. My loss of consciousness was so profound that I had no experience, none at all, of time passing, as one does during ordinary sleep. I went under, then seemed almost immediately to wake up. The hours between might as well not have been there.

If an anesthetic can do this, I thought afterwards, if it can so thoroughly cancel what I thought of as me, what will death be like? And this led me to wonder what I consider my self to be. Is it the sum of my memories? That could be canceled by a blood clot. Is what I consider my self, or my soul, what God considers my self? And could I imagine my self or my soul without a body that was unquestionably me, any more than I can consider my mind without my brain?

After ten years as a parish priest, after many conversations with parishioners and with other clergy, I am convinced that, where death and the afterlife are concerned, most Christians are functionally Neoplatonists. Neoplatonism influenced many early Christian thinkers, Augustine among them. They found the soul not only superior to the body, and an entity quite separate from the body, but they considered the body an encumbrance, something we will be happy to escape.

Think of the way many of us were taught: after death an immortal soul leaves the mortal body and goes to heaven or hell (or, if you are Roman Catholic, maybe — even probably — to purgatory). This thinking implies that we will be much happier once the soul leaves our body behind. Religion always gave a nod to the idea that resurrection was somehow part of this — we would get glorified bodies after the general resurrection at the end of time, and they wouldn't be much like bodies at all — but the really important thing was going to heaven after death. Much Christian writing and preaching about death implicitly denigrated the body and the flesh. In this view, the spirit is superior to flesh, and the soul, freed from the flesh, will certainly be better off.

We can see how some scripture passages could be read this way. "Who will deliver me from this body of death?" Paul asks in Romans (7:24). But for Paul, the sense of the flesh as a negative thing comes not from the fact that flesh is physical rather than spiritual, but from the fact that, as a result of sin, it is death-bearing. For Paul, the world, before God's will is completed in it, is given over to suffering and death, to the mystery represented by Christ's Passion and Cross. The problem is not with the physical, fleshly nature of our being. The problem, rather, is that the physical world and the flesh — both holy and good from the time of creation — have been dragged into sin and death by a spiritual, not physical, failing that we both choose and fall into, a dark possibility that infected the world from the moment we received the possibility of choice.

Orthodox theologian Alexander Schmemann cites Romans 5:12 — "Through death, sin has come into the world" — and comments that

> for Christianity, death first of all is revealed as part of the moral order, as a spiritual catastrophe. In some final and indescribable sense

man *desired death,* or perhaps one might say, he did not desire that life that was given to him by God freely, with love and joy. . . . The world is a perpetual revelation of God about himself to humanity; it is only a means of communion, of this constant, free, and joyful encounter with the only content of life — with the Life of life itself — with God. . . . But the tragedy — and herein lies the heart of the Christian teaching about sin — is that man did not desire this life with God and for God. He desired life *for himself,* and in himself he found the purpose, the goal, and the content of life. And in this free choice of himself, and not of God, in his preference for himself over God, without realizing it, man became inextricably a slave of the world, a slave of his own dependence on the world.[1]

Schmemann points out that even our life-sustaining eating is a communion with death. The plants we eat have been cut away from their roots, the fruit has been plucked from the tree, the animals have

1. Alexander Schmemann, *O Death, Where Is Thy Sting?* (Crestwood, NY: St. Vladimir's Seminary Press, 2003), pp. 33, 34-35.

been killed. "He eats in order to live, but with his food he communes with what is mortal, for food does not have life in itself. . . . Thus, death is the fruit of a life that is poisoned and perpetually disintegrating, a disintegration to which man has freely subjected himself. Not having life in himself, he has subjected himself to the world of death."[2]

If we put aside the assumptions we have been taught regarding death and life after death, the scriptures clearly show that the idea of an afterlife defined as the immortality of the soul is more a Neoplatonist than a Christian idea. Biblically, eternal life and resurrection are essentially the same thing. Resurrection implies embodiment. It means taking the flesh — God's creation, a good thing — more seriously than much of Christian thought has tended to. Second Maccabees presents resurrection dramatically. After torture, one of the persecuted brothers "quickly put out his tongue and courageously stretched forth his hands, and said nobly, 'I got these from Heaven, and because of his laws I disdain them, and from him I hope to get them back again'" (7:10-11). Isaiah even more explicitly links the body to immortality: "The dead shall live,

2. Schmemann, *O Death,* p. 35.

their bodies shall rise. O dwellers in the dust, awake and sing for joy!" (26:19).

But why does the Neoplatonist idea of the unencumbered soul's immortality remain so attractive? It is easier, in a way, to think that something naturally immortal inheres in us, to be freed by death. The idea of an immortal soul makes death seem less total, less thoroughly annihilating. And this is precisely where we move away from the Bible. *Ruah*, in Hebrew, and *pneuma*, in Greek, are often translated "spirit" but both literally mean "breath." "Put not your trust in princes, in a son of man, in whom there is no help," says Psalm 146. "When his breath departs he returns to his earth; on that very day his plans perish." Another psalm is more stark: "As for man, his days are like grass; he flourishes like a flower of the field;/for the wind passes over it, and it is gone,/and its place knows it no more" (Ps. 103). Biblically, death is precisely what you see. The corpse in front of you is not the husk of Fred, who has left a fleshly prison to go in some shining form to a better world. It is Fred, dead.

Belief in the immortality of the soul attracts us because we hope that something about us is less contingent than the body, less creaturely, something that possesses an inherent immortality. For much of history, people believed the mind was somehow separate from the body, consciousness was somehow spiritual in a way that the meat soup of the brain was not. Although philosophers and neurologists still debate the nature of the relationship between mind and brain, we no longer think that one can be in any way separate from the other.

But the idea of immortality has more to it than that. If we see our bodies as our selves, if we understand that soul and body are not separate entities but that the fullness of what we are spiritually can exist only embodied, then we are totally dependent on something that we do not control. While believers hold that God wills them into being from nothing, heartbeat by heartbeat, and that from the beginning of time God knew that we would exist and saw this as something good, we also know that before a certain point — our conception — we simply were not. It was God's will that brought us into being, and any being we have after death will likewise have to be willed by God. Our immortality has nothing to do with something we control or are due.

Belief in resurrection puts our faith more on the line than belief in an immortal soul. To believe in resurrection means that, just as we had no life before our conception, so we can have no life after death that is not given to us by God's willing it to be so. And we cannot know what any kind of life after death will be like or how it will be accomplished. This insults our imagined autonomy.

All of this means that we are putting ourselves completely into the hands of a God we cannot understand but can only trust. It is like stepping over the edge of a cliff in the dark, hoping that the promised net will be there — that what we have been told, secondhand, will be true. I say secondhand because even someone who thought he or she had witnessed the transfiguration or the resurrection of Christ might later legitimately wonder, might have second thoughts. Peter, after witnessing the transfiguration, denied Jesus three times. And none of us have come nearly that close to witnessing God's glory. Still, as believers we have a compelling story. We hold on to it because it makes more sense to us than any other story — more sense than reincarnation, or ultimate meaninglessness, or an extinction we won't have to worry about because we won't be there to experience it.

I am not sure I have resolved what I encountered in my experience of anesthesia, except to say that if I saw death as a cancellation, as total an ending as humans could experience (if total endings can actually be a matter of experience), then at the same time I knew God has the power to raise me to life. There may be no interim between death and resurrection.... When we die, we may be out of the space/time continuum, the "now" and "later" of the universe as we know it, with time as one of its limited dimensions. It may not make sense to speak of a period of time between death and resurrection. When we die we may find ourselves already resurrected, because in God's time it has all been accomplished. Jesus says to the thief, "Today you will be with me in paradise" (Luke 23:43). Is that "today" a particular twenty-four hour period more than two thousand years ago? Or is it the day of the Lord's triumph, when all will be as God has wanted it to be from the beginning of time?

This day of the Lord is pointed to in John 5:25: "Truly, truly, I say to you, the day is coming, and now is, when the dead will hear the voice of the Son of God, and those who hear will live." It is coming: We are moving towards the time in which it will all be accomplished; for us it has not happened yet. But in God's time it has already been accomplished: That is the Lord's joy, which we are invited to enter. The same sense of "already/not yet" is implicit in the Eucharist, where we take the bread of the kingdom that is still to come.

What does this do to the Orthodox tradition of praying to the saints, asking for their prayers? The dead we ask to pray for us are alive in a way we cannot imagine. Our faith is simply that God is the God of the living. In God all has been accomplished, and we pray, in a way, towards that time. As to how we get from here to there, I have no idea. But it will have everything to do with God's will, and nothing to do with anything I can imagine. My faith, finally, is that if I am canceled by the power death has in our world, then God's greater power can overcome it.

Is the desire to survive death, to live despite death, a case of wanting to believe in something because the alternative seems too bleak? Or, as some would have it, is this a case of not wanting to face the truth? Here one must ask why we would prefer the assumption that the truth will be bleak over good news to the contrary. I say this as one whose instincts are all agnostic, dark, and pessimistic; but I have experienced enough to know that I am often wrong in allowing those instincts to govern my assumptions. For instance, that lump turns out not to be cancerous, more often than not. But even apart from such obvious moments, the times when a great beauty or joy bursts in on you, or the incandescence of love overwhelms you, put darkness and pessimism in their lesser place. Either such experiences are merely human symptoms (like indigestion and dandruff), or they point to what the universe is about, its ultimate ground. Without proof — without proof being possible — I will try to live as if the latter were true.

The idea that the soul can exist — separate from the body, existing as a monad — is, if not part of orthodox Christian thought, a popular misunderstanding among Christians. We find it hard, especially in a culture that stresses individualism, to accept the idea that the self exists only in relationship. In fact, who we are is formed by the family we are born into, the language we learn, the culture we are immersed in. Finally, we are, we exist, because we are loved by God, who wills us to be. Even within the Trinity, the persons exist separately only in relation to one another. The moment we think that our being is in any way independent of relationship, we fall into the trap Genesis warned us about: We want to be like gods.

Please understand that in moving away from terms like "immortal soul" to a more biblical understanding, I do not mean that God wishes for us to be transitory or to say that we are not in fact called forth into eternal being. Rather, I mean only to move away from giving priority to the disembodied and the idea that what really matters is liberation from the flesh. To think that we can have an eternal life apart from resurrection is not Christian. It means taking neither death nor resurrection seriously enough, neither seeing the tragedy of the first in all its depth nor the great joy of the second in all its glory.

First of all, we must take seriously the tragedy of death. Christian belief does not reconcile us with death but helps us see it for the horror it is. Jesus weeps at the tomb of Lazarus, and at Gethsemane he is filled with horror at what awaits him. Contrast this with forms of religion that console us with the idea that "death is just a part of life." Some part. We must face the fact that death is as bad as it looks and is not a simple rite of passage. Death is the loss of everything we have known. No one who has loved anyone or anything in this life can find the idea of leaving life anything but tragic.

The Christian finds joy in the fact that even this enemy, even this thing we fear most — and rightly so — has been overcome in Christ. The Paschal liturgy of the Orthodox Church sings over and over again, "Christ is risen from the dead, trampling down death by death, and upon those in the tombs bestowing life." It is a victory dance. And it involves embodiment. Schmemann says:

> In essence, my body is my relationship to the world, to others; it is my life as communion and as mutual relationship. Without exception, everything in the body, in the human organism, is created for this relationship, for this communion, for this coming out of oneself. It is not an accident, of course, that love, the highest form of communion, finds its incarnation in the body; the body is that which sees, hears, feels, and thereby leads me out of the isolation of my I. . . . [T]he body is not the darkness of the soul, but rather the body is its freedom, for the body is the soul as love, the soul as communion, the soul as life, the soul as movement. And this is why, when the soul loses the body, when it is separated from the body, it loses life; it dies, even if this dying of the soul is not a complete annihilation, but a dormition, or sleep.[3]

3. Schmemann, *O Death,* pp. 42-43.

What will this sleep of the soul be like? Who knows, or can? We should allow ourselves — in fact, should demand of ourselves — an agnosticism about imagining the afterlife or what resurrection will mean. Our best scriptural witnesses stammer. Paul, in 1 Corinthians 15, speaks of the body we now have as a mere kernel, as if what it will blossom into is something we are incapable of imagining. In 1 John 3:2 we are told, "Beloved, we are God's children now; it does not yet appear what we shall be, but we know that when he appears we shall be like him, for we shall see him as he is."

Christianity turned the ancient idea of life after death on its head. Belief in resurrection was only a slowly dawning sense in Hebrew scripture. The world of 1 Samuel, with the story of Saul's visit to the medium at Endor to call up the spirit of Samuel, is not far from the world of Homer and the ancient Greeks. Sheol and Hades were places in which the dead were truly "shadows of their former selves," shades. Earth is where life is truly lived. After death only faint echoes live on. The concept of resurrection that we read about in Ezekiel, Isaiah, and Maccabees has moved beyond the earlier idea of death as a passage from firm reality into a dreamy land of shadows.

In Luke the angels at the tomb of Jesus say to the disciples, who expected to see Jesus' body, "Why do you seek the living among the dead?" (24:5). Resurrected life, far from being shadowy and ethereal, is more real, more truly alive, than we are capable of knowing on this side of death. Belief in resurrection inverts the usual ancient model: Now we are the shades, and this wounded world resembles the Sheol or Hades of the ancients' imagining. We are called to expect a life that our understanding cannot yet encompass, a wider life that goes from one depth of glory to another, forever.

Of course, it is hard to have faith that this will be so. But as Daniel Callahan suggests, some secular approaches to the idea of immortality are even more problematic. For example, Callahan addresses the scientific vision of life extension, which encompasses even the idea of extending life forever, and contrasts it with the Christian approach to the question of eternal life. He quotes professor of religion Carol Zaleski: "To be given everlasting longevity without being remade for eternal life is to live under a curse."[4] Callahan goes on to point out

4. Daniel Callahan, "Visions of Eternity," *First Things,* May, 2003, p. 31.

what is obvious to us, but which is not as apparent as it should be to optimistic proponents of life extension. Human behavior, not a conquerable biology, makes death and suffering the agonies they are: "Is a death from cancer at eighty worse than death at the same age in a concentration camp from murder or deliberate starvation? Or is death at age five from a genetic disease worse than death from a nuclear bomb? Or is the pain of a broken marriage, or spousal abuse, or child molestation, necessarily less than the pain of arthritis or congestive heart failure?"[5] The extension of human life in all its weakness, for many years or forever, would mean extending nearly infinite forms of misery, heartlessness, boredom, and torment, most of them the results of the kind of people we are.

Because Christian belief holds that eternal life requires embodiment, Christianity has a long tradition of thought about what eternal embodiment might mean. It would mean a transformed reality participated in by a transformed people. Callahan offers a delightful quote from Marguerite of Oingt, a fourteenth century nun and mystic, who wrote that

5. Callahan, "Visions of Eternity," p. 31.

the saints will be completely within their Creator as the fish within the sea; they will drink to satiety, without getting tired and without in any way diminishing the water. . . . [They] will drink and eat the great sweetness of God. And the more they eat, the more their hunger will grow. And this sweetness cannot decrease any more or less than can the water of the sea.[6]

So much for the problem of boredom. Marguerite's metaphor is very much like the vision of St. Gregory of Nyssa, who said that because God is infinitely other than we are, an eternity of approaching what we can never reach will mean continual transformation.

We can conceive then of no limitation in an infinite nature; and that which is limitless cannot by its nature be understood. And so every desire for the Beautiful which draws us on in this ascent is intensified by the soul's very progress towards it. And this is the real

6. Callahan, "Visions of Eternity," p. 33.

meaning of seeing God: never to have this desire satisfied.[7]

Christian thinkers have approached the idea of immortality in a way that is, in Callahan's words, a "much richer, more nuanced picture than anything the scientists and their followers have conjured up." He quotes Caroline Walker Bynum's book, *The Resurrection of the Body:*

> However absurd the idea of resurrection may seem, "it is a concept of sublime courage and optimism. It locates redemption there where ultimate horror also resides — in pain, mutilation, death, and decay.... Those who articulated [it] faced without flinching the most negative of all the consequences of embodiment: the fragmentation, slime, and stench of the grave.... [W]e may not find their solutions plausible, but it is hard to feel they got the problem wrong."

Callahan comments:

7. Gregory of Nyssa, *From Glory to Glory* (Crestwood, NY: St. Vladimir's Seminary Press, 1979), pp. 147-48.

The crux of their "courage and optimism" was to make the body the center of their attention, turning their back on the Greek notion that the soul is the essence of personhood. Not so, the medievals held: it is the body.[8]

Callahan is bold enough to suggest that scientists might pay more attention to the Christian vision, much as it might gall them to take seriously a tradition they too often see as hostile to science: "Nonetheless, in the doctrine of the resurrection of the body many generations of thoughtful and imaginative people have tried to imagine what eternal life might be like; and, even more to the point, what it *ought* to be like if we are sensibly to desire it."[9]

And we do desire it, sensibly or not so sensibly. Having been given the vision of a God whose care for us is so heartbreakingly thorough that he became one of us, suffering what we suffer, dying as we do, to show us that even what we fear most has been conquered by a love we are called to show one another, we can't help but hope that it is true and

8. Callahan, "Visions of Eternity," p. 33.
9. Callahan, "Visions of Eternity," p. 34.

try to stake our lives on that hope. Our faith tells us that we have been baptized into Christ's death and the hope of resurrection. "For you have died," Colossians tells us, "and your life is hid with Christ in God. When Christ who is our life appears, then you also will appear with him in glory" (3:3-4). This is the risen Christ who asked Mary not to cling to him, who showed Thomas wounds received on our side of death, and who made breakfast for his friends at the edge of the sea. And if we find this hard to believe, let us hope that our doubt has something in common with that of the apostles when they encountered the risen Christ: "While they still disbelieved for joy and wondered, he said to them, 'Have you anything here to eat?'" (Luke 24:41).